How to Sell Your Film:
Interviews about Marketing with Successful Indie Filmmakers

Written by Nathan March

How to Sell Your Film: Interviews about Marketing with Successful
Indie Filmmakers

Written by Nathan March

Published by Follow Magazine

Introduction

Hello, filmmaker. Your work makes an enormous contribution to people's lives. I'm sure you have days of self-doubt and days when you can conquer the world. My passion is that creative work is elevated to ever-higher status in society. To that end, over the last two years, I have interviewed dozens of filmmakers, writers, musicians, and visual artists to find out how they have made sure their work connects with their audience. That's right, I'm talking marketing and promotion.

This book features interviews with ten successful filmmakers. Its intention is to give you a real inside view on how to market your film. Indie filmmaker, Brooks Elms, once said to me that, "WAY more people see the marketing of a film, than ever see the film itself. Perhaps the ratio is even 30 to 1. Maybe 50 to 1. Or more. So why NOT make the marketing awesome?"

Of course, marketing and promotion, on their own, don't build a sustainable film career. As I've talked to filmmakers and other creatives over the last two years, I've found that there are three common elements to a successful career. Every artist, author, musician, and filmmaker that I've spoken with shares these three fundamentals. All of these creatives have spent years building up the skills and expertise to produce work of exceptional quality that adds meaning and substance to the lives of people that have contact with it. They all have an abiding commitment to creativity that has outlasted years of poverty, the judgement of friends and family, and battles with despair and depression. The third and final element is that they have all found a way to spread the word about their work beyond their immediate sphere of influence.

The cover of this book is, perhaps, a little ambiguous. I used the image of smoke partly obscuring some bloke in the desert partly because it's a striking image, partly because it looks like it's on a film set, but mostly because it reminds me of the phrase 'smoke and mirrors'. To a lot of people, that's what marketing is, the smoke and mirrors used to obscure the truth in a magic show.

There's a sense that marketing takes elements of what's real and puts a spin on it to make it more attractive to people that wouldn't normally buy a product. There may be some truth to that view but, for me, what that means is that we need to work even harder and unleash all of our creative skills to develop marketing strategies and material that interacts with our potential audience in a way that authentically represents our work. The poor reputation that marketing has doesn't mean we can give up on it altogether. Let's find the best, most honest examples of film marketing we can to get our work in front of the audience that wants to love it.

As artists, we often find it uncomfortable pushing our work out into the world. It feels dirty. It feels like we're selling out - putting material concerns above the pure value of creativity and art. I'd like to reframe that. If our work is going to have the impact that we want it to, if we are going to allow our creative work to spin gold in people's lives, people need to know about it. It's still uncomfortable but if we keep our eye on the goal of influencing individuals through our art, we have to find ways of promoting ourselves and our work.

These interviews give you the chance to see the business practices of other filmmakers to learn how they are using social media and other avenues to promote their work. Along the way, you will get to know eleven remarkable artists who are creating important work that is thoughtful, unique, and impressive.

I hope this book gives you inspiration and information to make today a world-conquering day for you!

Alex Ferrari

Chapter 1 Alex Ferrari

Alex is based in the US and has a number of strings to his bow. Every creative spirit has its inception somewhere. Alex started -

… as a tape-dubber in Miami and then turned into an editor. I did commercial work as an editor and feature work in Miami. Then I opened up my own post-production company. From there I directed a short that was fairly successful. I sold over five thousand DVDs of that by myself. We made the movie for about eight grand so we generated almost ninety thousand dollars doing that in two thousand and five. It was very successful. I parlayed that into shooting a few more films. That started my commercial directing career so I'm shooting commercials, music videos, things like that. I moved to LA about eight years ago and here I built up my post-production company, Numb Robot. Most recently I opened up the way I hope to pay it forward to future generations of filmmakers IndieFilmHustle.com where I teach people how to survive and thrive in the crazy film business.

In independent film, it often feels like there are barriers to reaching the next level, getting the next project up. What advice does Alex have for breaking through?

…I've been pounding my head against the wall for 20 years so I feel you. I think that as filmmakers we're always looking for permission to make a movie. We're looking for someone to go, "you may direct, you may tell your story as a filmmaker". And that is what we've been sold since we went to film school. It's a lie now more than ever. There are tools available for you to go out and make your movie. Now the question is what are you willing to do to get to that next level. To tell a good story to make a good movie takes time. It takes time, energy, and it's not something that gets done in a couple of weeks. What happens when filmmakers are done with that process? They're exhausted. They're done. "Okay, now I'm going to send it out to a few festivals and hope that I get discovered. Somebody will pick it up and give me money for it". That's not the reality. There's so much gluttony of product out there, bad product.

When you start writing the script you have to understand that the end of the movie is not when you've done editing. The end of the movie is when you've sold it. It's gone. You've made your money and you can move on to the next project. At the end of editing, it's 50% of the way. That's the way I look at it. There's another year to a year and a half of promotion, marketing, sales. Now if you're able to build up a community that loves what you do and you're able to sell to that community then this process becomes a little easier.

When Alex distributed his film, Broken, Twitter was but an impossible dream and Instagram wasn't even a twinkle in the eye. MySpace was huge (remember MySpace?) and Facebook was just one year old. Whatever the social media landscape and whatever strategy you use, creativity is the key. Alex is an energetic filmmaker and he brings that same energy to his marketing approach.

...I just instinctively went after where the people were. So I went after message boards, I went after every news organisation that talked and reviewed indie films I had a pretty kick ass trailer that we put together to promote the movie. That trailer got so much play it wasn't even funny. We even got the world famous film critic Roger Ebert (rest in peace). He gave us a review which was unheard of for a short film of our stature.

Sometimes the audience isn't willing to hand over cash for certain creative products. If it's important to you to have a paying audience you could consider packaging your art with another related product that people are willing to pay for.

...what I did was, when I made the movie I wanted to sell it but I knew that there was no way that the general public would pay me money for a twenty-minute short film with no actors with any names in it from a first time director. I consciously decided to market it to a niche audience that I knew would buy it: independent filmmakers. I could maybe have a few people buy the short but a lot of people would be interested in how I made it. Before I made the movie I started looking for information about how to make an independent film. I could not find a DVD, nothing, because everything was always, you know, commentaries by Martin Scorcese.

Everything was aimed at these big budget movies. Nobody was talking about how to make a movie in your home. No one thought about that. I thought, there's something missing in the marketplace. I'm going to create a movie that showed off a lot of technical prowess. I put together a full DVD on how we made it, what it took to make it. I put it all together and I started marketing it online myself. I just marketed the heck out of it and that was the key, branding, and marketing.

It doesn't matter how much marketing you do if your product doesn't connect with people. Art is about eliciting emotion. That's why we do it right?

People really got a lot out of it. When I opened up Indie Film Hustle all these Broken fans started coming out of the woodwork and people were like "I remember you, I saw your movie ten years ago". "It really helped me, thank you so much". As an artist, you really feel humbled by something like that. That's how I was able to sell it back then and am still selling it today.

The art has to be good but the quality of the product is irrelevant if no one gets to hear about it. You can't just rely on the product to sell itself, can you?

No, because without the show there ain't no business but without the business, there is definitely no show. Being a filmmaker, it's a very expensive medium to express yourself and if you don't understand the business side of it, you'll be eaten alive. A lot of filmmakers go after the dream, "Harvey Weinstein is going to discover me and give me millions of dollars and I'm just going to direct the movies that I want into the happy sunset". You know, it doesn't work. It's not a business plan. It's the equivalent of me opening up a burger joint and going, "I'm going to be the next McDonalds". It doesn't work that way. So when filmmakers start thinking about making a more sustainable life as opposed to following the dream you have to build a more sustainable business model. Meaning, how can I make a living doing my art. So what do I have to do? How much do I need to make in a year to sustain myself as an artist? The way the world works today with selling your work directly to consumers without having distributors or middle men you can build your community directly and sell to that community.

It doesn't happen overnight. Look at all these YouTube guys that just get millions of followers and they're making advertising revenue and selling t-shirts and they have this raving fan of communities that follow them because they're doing whatever they're doing but their fans love what they're doing. As an artist there are ways of making a living, it's a matter of getting your mindset to a point where you go okay so what do I need to survive, you know? For me, not just to survive but to thrive.

Indie Film Hustle is Alex's new platform to give indie filmmakers the tools to create a sustainable business. It's already making waves across the social sphere. How does Alex connect with his community?

…I use GetResponse as my email list host. I found for my size list it made sense. It's not a huge list at the moment. Once you start getting into a hundred thousand people, fifty thousand, that's when you might need a little bit more sophistication as far as funnels and automation, almost AI technology. I use HootSuite for some posting. Not a lot of HootSuite but I use them when I post some stuff just to save time and then everything else is kinda old school. The thing with social media as a general statement is you wanna pick one or two that work for you. I'm seeing what works. I'm going okay well this kind of thing works I'm getting a lot of traction out of this and I didn't get a lot of traction out of this. I'm learning as I go along. My top three are Instagram, Twitter, and Facebook. Those are the ones that generate the most traffic for me. If you're a cooking blog, Pinterest is where you should be. If you're hitting 18 to 25-year-olds, you gotta be on Tumblr. If they're not working for you just don't do them. Facebook is great and I generate a lot of traffic from Facebook. It's a great way that I interact with my community. I've become a huge Instagram guy. I love Instagram, it's very, very powerful. It's immediate feedback, it's very easy to get followers there as long as you have a good feed.

We all know that art requires space, boredom, inspiration. How does Alex feed his filmmaking habit?

From the movies I watch. My church is a movie theatre, alone in a movie theatre, literally sometimes.

When I was younger I would just go if my life was tough I'd go find a good movie, sit down, and escape. By the time the movie was over a lot of times, my problem might still be there but I might have different perspective on it or I might be inspired to do something else. That's the power of cinema.

Alex Ferrari and Indie Film Hustle can be found all over the socials. His podcast is a great place to familiarise yourself with all things indie film. Connect with Alex at indiefilmhustle.com.

Kirsty Stark

Chapter 2 Kirsty Stark

Kirsty Stark moved from working in the camera department on sets to producing projects in Australia for the big and small screen. Her first big project for the small screen was a three-minute prologue to a web series, Wastelander Panda.

Initially, it was just intended to be put online as something to show to our friends and family and the idea just started spreading and so we did some work to help it along. It ended up having over a hundred thousand views in the first three days, way beyond any of our expectations.

It's crazy exciting when something takes off like that. It can be hard to turn off.

The first night we slept and we said, we'll see what happens in the morning when we wake up and it was good. Because of the American time difference, we got a huge spike overnight and it went from about a thousand or two thousand views up to ten thousand and then from that point, it just kept growing. It was actually on Australia Day and I remember the three of us were at this Australia Day party and we were sitting on our phones in the corner hitting refresh watching the counters keep going up. It was a pretty exciting time.

From Australia to the United States, Wastelander Panda made its mark on the sci-fi scene.

It traveled pretty far. We got on the front page of Buzzfeed which wasn't as huge as it is now but it still had the advantage of viewers from all over the world and those people helped to spread it in their own communities as well. I think that hundred thousand views were spread over about fifty-two different countries, which is one of the advantages of getting on a major site.

Kirsty recently released her first feature film, A Month of Sundays. With such a huge following from Wastelander Panda does that mean that A Month of Sundays had an automatic audience?

Not really, partly because A Month of Sundays is a completely different project aimed at a forty-five plus female skewed audience, whereas, Wastelander Panda was really the 18 to 35-year-old male audience. There didn't really seem to be that much to bring them along.

Does that mean that the Wastelander Panda audience is lost forever?

Another project I'm working on, Goober, is back in that younger space, we may try and attract some of that Wastelander Panda audience across. There's some audiences that do cross over like the local film community obviously and people that know what's happening in the state but in terms of that sci-fi audience, we didn't really do a lot of work to get them interested in A Month of Sundays.

Of course, the Wastelander Panda team collected some email addresses along the way.

We ran a Pozzible campaign and captured a lot of email addresses which is how our mailing list started and then we tried to capture email addresses through our website along the way. We had an interactive website where you could go and explore the world of the Wasteland through a map which is pretty cool. For the most part, it was social media so we've got a much bigger Facebook following than we do mailing list. We did run some competitions and things like that to transfer them but I think people in that younger audience prefer to be engaged on social media than to open an email.

Sometimes engaging with your audience can take a project in a different direction.

If our online audience didn't exist the project wouldn't have ever happened. I think the main thing was that we originally wanted to go to TV. That was our initial plan for the series. Once we realised through the prologue what an audience we had online and how releasing online would allow us to access that worldwide audience that was the direction we took instead of trying to go straight to a TV series.

The crowdfunding campaign, as well, really proved to the South Australian Film Corporation that we had an audience out there. That was our way of accessing further financing from them as well, by breaking down all the statistics of our viewers, where they came from, where they heard about us, how much they were investing already through the crowdfunding campaign.

Statistics. The world revolves around numbers, but it can be difficult sometimes to find the numbers and make them presentable in pitch documents.

It was pretty rough at the time. We did a lot of just going into the Vimeo and YouTube backend. They have their basic breakdowns. We also went into the marketing and sponsorship details of all of the websites we were featured on. Buzzfeed has a 'sponsor us' section in tiny text down the bottom corner because they try to hide it from the public. They've got a breakdown which says this is how many times we're accessed daily and this is where people live. We used that to create an overall picture of who our audience was and said well we got fifty thousand views from this website and this is their demographic and so we assume that our demographic falls into that.

After the prologue, the Wastleander Panda team released three Wastelander Panda short films online. They were then commissioned by Australia's national broadcaster, the ABC, to produce a short series based on the same material. This was broadcast on the ABCs online platform, iView. Getting information about your audience from a broadcaster is different to YouTube or Vimeo.

That was a lot harder because it's all internal there and they seem to have less detailed information on their platform than YouTube or Vimeo do. We were able to get general statistics but nothing as detailed as what we'd done ourselves. I'm not sure whether they couldn't access it or they only provided us with the general stuff.

These days there is a myriad of tools and apps that make it easier for artists to connect with their audience. What tools does Kirsty use?

I'm one of those people that just goes onto Facebook and just types it in.

I do use the scheduling tool but Ella McIntire who ran most of our social media for Wastelander Panda is really on top of all that stuff and I know she was using Hootsuite and probably quite a few different apps throughout the process as well.

So Ella McIntyre was in charge of the socials?

We called her our Producer of Digital Distribution, which is a film world term for social outreach. Throughout the shoot, she was collecting behind the scenes footage and collecting interviews with cast and crew. She collaborated with our stills photographer to make sure there were elements that we could add text to and release as memes or little advertising images. We wanted enough content to keep audiences entertained throughout all of those times where there's not really a lot going on apart from people sitting in front of the computer. Occasionally our VFX guys would all put on the panda heads and sit in front of the computers and we'd just take a snapshot in the office. We tried to keep people engaged in the journey and knowing what we were up to without just going, "today we did visual effects".

How many creatives would give up their right hand to have someone running their social media for them? Where do you find someone like that?

She wasn't involved when we did the prologue. She's a friend of ours and we went around to her house that first night when it had gone online and it was starting to get some traction. She basically said, "what are you doing with this?" We were like, "what do you mean what are you doing we've already put it online", and she started giving us this detailed breakdown of how all of the blogs and aggregator sites are linked on the Internet. This was all just through her own personal knowledge she'd never worked at a social media company or anything. She just spent a lot of time on the internet and paid attention to how it all worked. It also helped that Wastelander Panda was the kind of content that she watched and so she already went to those sites and understood their culture. You can't just go bashing into a sci-fi website if, like me, you've never spent any time there and understood how it works. She was the target demographic. She's got a really good intuition for how it all works.

To find out more about the marketing and distribution models developed and exploited by Kirsty Stark and the rest of the Wastelander Panda team look for their excellent series of podcasts on the Hope in Film website.

Kirsty can be found online at www.epicfilms.com.au

Jen Finelli & Samantha Mauney

Chapter 3 Jen Finelli & Samantha Mauney

Jen Finelli and Samantha Mauney are filmmakers. Their film I'm Having an Affair With My Wife! is in pre-production but it's already making waves. This story isn't your typical Rom Com.

We're passionate because we have a mission for ourselves. I'm a heavy-set girl of mixed heritage. My producer, Sam, is a nerdy Black woman with a linguistics degree. We're both married. To put it bluntly, we don't see leads like ourselves in romance. We see skinny blonde singles held up as the sole ideal of beauty, and we think it's time to stop telling young girls that's the only desirable female self. I wrote this film because I want to see a plus-size Black girl make it in love. And, as an Asian-American, I want Asians playing non-stereotyped leads. Where are the good films about falling in love with your spouse, anyway? We're here because no one else is.

Now that sounds interesting! Can you tell us more about the film?

Lashonda's a driven, successful businesswoman with a passion for Korean food (and Korean men). Sung-min's a laid-back artist who loves good music as much as he loves to kick back with a comic book.
When their marriage goes sour, they both seek out affairs online--and accidentally end up secretly dating each other.
Pina Colada song in real life, this quirky new film explores the things we're really married to—like our work, our hobbies, our habits, and our preferences—and the ways it can be fun and fulfilling to cheat on them. (What does that even mean, right?) It's a celebration of marriage that doesn't hide from the problems with happily ever after, and it's slated to film summer of 2018!

I've heard a rumour that you're crowdfunding now on Seed and Spark, is that right?

Folks who pledge $30 or more get free tickets to a sweet indie film launch party. You can't get that later! As well as the crowdfunding page, visit www.mysweetaffair.com for updates, marriage "cheats," and an ongoing conversation about diversity and representation in movies. So yeah, good stuff. Representing diversity and ladies in film, woo!

What is it about these women that make them (and their films) unique?

We're unique because, as we described above, we're making funnies with a mission that you just don't see in a lot of Hollywood today. We're also unique because we're a linguist and, in four months, a doctor. We've had a ton of odd life experiences that pour into what we do--experiences a lot of other people haven't had. Like hanging out with prostitutes, Senators, and a former gang leader, or working on film sets with Denzel Washington and Michael Bay. Combined, we have more weird stories about exploring tropical islands and hanging out with dead languages and dead people than any other indie filmmakers out there.
We're adventurers, and we're looking forward to having our next adventure with YOU.

Do you promote your work on social media? What platforms are you on?

Sam socials
www.samanthamauney.com/
www.twitter.com/samanthamauney

Film socials
Site: www.mysweetaffair.com
www.twitter.com/affair_movie
www.facebook.com/HavingAnAffairWithMyWife

Jen socials
www.twitter.com.petr3pan
Scifi: www.byjenfinelli.com
Comics character kills his author: www.becominghero.ninja

On which platform do you have the largest audience?

Twitter! We went from 0 to almost 2000 in five months. We've really focused on reciprocity, and we give all of our followers a chance to get our awesome indie filmmakers' resource guide!

How have you grown your social media audience?

We make sure to follow the rules we learned from a lot of Buffer and Twitter analytics math research, rules like:
-Always two hashtags. Never more, never less.
-Always @ mention someone if you can.
-Use www.analytics.twitter.com to check all your performances.
-Use dlvr.it and other feeds to trawl the web for news.
-Have someone on your team use Roundteam so they can RT your tweets (some of our followers have discovered our film account through my slightly larger social media account)
-And, our newest one, use Wordpress plug-ins like Microblogposter and Re-post Old Post to keep your evergreen content circling on Twitter.

Actually, we have a whole podcast about marketing resources--it's an hour-long breakdown of the things we've discovered that rock! Tons and tons of things to give away to creators. www.mysweetaffair.com/indie-film-marketing

If there was one thing readers should know about social media marketing what would it be?

You can only get good at one social media at a time. We chose Twitter because it works for film, but your Google rank improves if you use MORE socials: every time a social points to your site, your rank improves. So we use Blog2Social to post to all the socials at once, even the ones we're not super-good at. Use Blog2Social if you've got a Wordpress site!

Do you pay for advertising either online or in other media?

Not really. We've dropped a few cents on Facebook ads. But we're really excited about starting to use Project Wonderful! You can actually see Project Wonderful running on my comics site, if you disable ads, and you can click under the ad to run your own ad there.
We like the structure Project Wonderful offers for creators, where you bid on spots and pay based on days your ad is shown. Pretty cool.

Where do you make the most sales?

We've had some money love dropped on the donations page of our website at www.mysweetaffair.com.

Do you have any techniques to convert followers into customers?

Yup! Our landing page and our welcome Tweet have been called "marketing genius" by strangers we didn't know. It's sent by StatusBrew. People hate DMs, so we don't do that. But this is a friendly, authentic welcome Tweet, and people like it, Click the link in the welcome Tweet, and you end up on our awesome page where we give away cool stuff to people! We're always thinking up new things to give away there. It's what's called Inbound Marketing, and it's basically the idea that if you give away real value for free (not "free*") then people will come back to buy your actual stuff. I've got a little post about Inbound Marketing software here actually. www.petrepan.blogspot.com/2013/06/inbound-marketing-which-software.html
But the point is, convert followers to customers by always giving them cool things!

Do you have a marketing philosophy?

If you're generous, you'll be rewarded. We exist to give. We give to our viewers, we give to our followers, and when our film's done, it will give to the film community as a whole.

You've already mentioned some of the tools and apps you use. Do you have any tips on which tools are best?

Definitely, check out the tools I've already mentioned and the marketing podcast above! We talk about the difference between Hootsuite and Buffer there a lot.

What are your top 3 tips to help other creative people learning to market their work?

First, your work has to not suck. A lot of times we think we're ready to show our stuff to the world when we're really not. I was subbing my sci-fi out like I was some big shot professional when I was what, fifteen, writing 500,000-word novels that sucked? Find a critique group, and become active in your craft, and then through those same groups, you'll find friends and then followers. Sam, our producer, rocks because she gets on every single set she can, in any capacity necessary: she doesn't care if she's an extra or the producer. And because she doesn't have a big ego thing holding her back, she gets a lot of awesome experience and learning she wouldn't otherwise have.

So be willing to put in the work. Be willing to stay up later, and delete your drafts, and start over again and again.

Second tip? Be giving, when you do get fans. Don't hold back. I got a great opportunity to do this podcast about crowdfunding because, at the moment when Tyler asked me why I chose Indiegogo, I didn't let myself see him as a competitor and stay greedy. www.comixlaunch.com/session080

Unbeknownst to him, I did all this intense mathematical research about Indiegogo so I could publish it on my site and get a bunch of views, but when he asked about it, I decided to share it with him. We ended up teaming up, and I got more attention than I otherwise would have. Don't let yourself be greedy. Share! I learned that from either Michael Hyatt or one of the other business blogs I follow.

The third tip, be consistent. I'm watching Rhett and Link's 1000 videos Youtube celebration, and it's got the same magic that Penny Arcade comics, or Black Nerd Girl's huge Twitter account, or any of these other big internet celebrities have. That's the magic of showing up on time. This is something I need to work on, but Sam is really good at it. Every Monday she's got something for you guys on our site, whether that's a podcast or a blog post from one of us. Consistency keeps people coming back.

It doesn't develop an audience as quickly as some fancy marketing technique, but it's what develops an audience that stays.

Now that's some great marketing advice! If you want more from Jen and Samantha check out their site, and follow them on the socials. And definitely, definitely, definitely take a look at their Seed and Spark campaign. Rewards start from $1 and just by clicking follow they receive real support. www.mysweetaffair.com

Lara Damiani

Chapter 4 Lara Damiani

Lara Damiani is a documentary filmmaker from Adelaide, Australia who travels the world to tell stories. She has a particular passion for global development. I began by asking Lara whether she has a marketing budget.

The only time I actually spent money on marketing outside of myself trying to do something was last year. I paid a writer to rewrite the content on my website. Other than that it's just me thinking, "okay, well how do you market with no budget?"

As with many independent filmmakers, social media is crucial for Lara's marketing and networking.

I use LinkedIn. What has been working for me on LinkedIn is making personal connections and letting people know what I do and why I do it and when I'm available. So I use LinkedIn and I'm still trying to work out, I guess, the best ways to do that.

In fact, I first came across Lara on LinkedIn and was impressed with the articles she wrote and her consistent presence. You wouldn't be reading this interview if it wasn't for Lara's work on LinkedIn. How, exactly, does Lara promote herself across this network? Does she have an article-publishing schedule that she works to?

No, not really. I've tried to. I don't think it's how my head works. There is information available on best times to post, best places to post and I can't stand that much structure. I try not to read too much of this because it's all so overwhelming.

Well then, how does Lara decide what to publish and when?

I posted an article just before you got here. I was reading the Guardian this morning and a journalist wrote this great story about deforestation. That's the big issue that I'm kind of passionate about. I did some work with a photojournalist in Malaysia and the Philippines and I thought, "I'll push that". I will use the journalist's heading and quote his article and put the video that we made for our project and hook that up there. It's that random.

What sort of articles does she like to publish on LinkedIn?

I'm publishing more now than I was. I realized. I like the fact that you can write pretty short punchy articles and then you can add something visual with them.

Lara has over one-thousand-four-hundred connections on LinkedIn. Most of those connections are people that are valuable for her work.

When I first got onto LinkedIn my connections were quite random. And then I started exploring LinkedIn to use it more effectively. Now I'm very specific about doing my own research about a person and what they're doing and whether we have something in common. Too often, I'll get these requests to connect from other people that are so random and have no connection.

Often social media can feel impersonal. How has Lara worked around that vibe on LinkedIn?

I've started using InMail rather than that bland 'I want to connect with you'. Sometimes I'll not necessarily know someone but I have a connection with them because of what they've done, so I'll ask them if they want to connect. I'm always quite specific about the reason I'm doing it.

And does that work? Do people engage?

I just got a response back yesterday from a lady who works in climate change adaptation in Kyrgyzstan. She's working on a big project that might have the need for some videos for evaluation so that could be an opportunity to work together. I guess I'm trying to be really specific about people that are either working in development communications or monitoring and evaluation where there is a component of visual evaluation or a need for an impact film or impact documentary.

It's so important to know what you do and how that suits your market. Lara has built up a solid business over a number of years. I asked her what factors have contributed to her success?

I think probably more than anything it's some stubborn sort of persistence. The thing is (and I know everyone says it), just loving what you're doing and believing in it. I think probably the one area where it's difficult on your own is to maintain that sense of self-worth and that sense of, "I can keep going". I think, especially on your own, it's difficult when you see what everyone else is doing. You know when you are working for yourself it's not about the income but it's more about the other aspects.

A good way of maintaining self-worth and deriving sustenance is...

finding other like-minded people. That's one thing that I'm trying to do more of. I'm producing, directing, shooting, editing, funding, it's all too much now so I'm trying to find other people to collaborate with and that's happening so that's a big thing. But also, finding other like-minded people just to share ideas with, run things past. It's huge for people working on their own.

Social media is a great way of finding other filmmakers to connect with.

The photojournalist from America that I got together with to work with on the rainforest project in Malaysia, that connection was through Facebook. I was just following him on Facebook. I loved his work and I remember saying one day I'd love to work with you on something and this came up. It wasn't a paid project we just paid for ourselves and said let's do this. Now we communicate by Skype and email and we can talk to each other and will run ideas past and we're trying to get a project up and running at the moment so we have a lot of that collaboration. Other people that I'm connected with on Facebook, we might ask each other information about the equipment we're using etc.

I asked Lara where she gets her leads from for future work.

Some Relief International work came directly through LinkedIn. I do some local work here and most of that is word of mouth; I don't even know how it started. Often they are ideas that I will try to make happen.

The Sight For All work is because, about three years ago, I was reading The Australian and there was this awesome article about Dr. James Yuki who is an ophthalmologist from Adelaide who had just come back from Burma or Myanmar. He's set up a charity and they're working in developing countries. I contacted him and said, "if you ever need help from a documentary filmmaking point of view I put my hand up". I eventually did a trip with him last year to Bangladesh and Vietnam where I followed him and I filmed him in surgery and training with some of the doctors.

Lara understands the area of international development that she's working in and has leveraged off that knowledge to really find ways she can make her offering as valuable as possible to the organizations she works with.

Often with NGOs, they don't have huge budgets and so the travel component of getting somewhere is quite restrictive. So, for example, I was in Bangladesh for Sight For All and prior to that I had connected up, through LinkedIn, with the country director of Relief International in Bangladesh. I said, "look, I'm going to be there" and he said, "well, we need a particular project done" and so I made a film for them while I was there. I try and make that efficiency where I can if I happen to be somewhere and I know someone might need something. It's easy for me just to stay on and do that work.

Lara has built up a great body of work and a solid reputation over a number of years. To find out more take a look at www.thinkfilms.com.au

Chris Kamen

Chapter 5 Chris Kamen

Chris Kamen is a film producer and entertainment lawyer who hails from Melbourne, Australia. His recent project Small Is Beautiful: A Tiny House Documentary *is one of those rare breeds of film: profitable.*

The film was a micro-budget so it didn't cost much to make. I think that's a big part of the secret - just not to spend much money in the first place.

How do you create a micro-budget film?

It was mainly Jeremy (Beasley) as a one-man band, shooting himself, doing all of his own sound and lighting. He's a very, very resourceful filmmaker, spending a lot of time in Portland in Oregon, which is the epicenter of the tiny house scene in the States. We spent months there following characters in a really intimate way, going about the struggles and the trials and tribulations of building the house.

And what exactly does micro-budget mean?

It only cost sixty grand to make and then we probably spent about thirty grand distributing it with some support from Screen Australia. We got some support from others along the way. Airbnb sponsored our launch. This is all publicly available via our case study. We decided to make all our numbers transparent as much as we can.
www.smallbeautifulmovie.com/blog/micro-budget-documentary-c

A small budget is one thing but you still need some audience to recoup your costs. Chris and Jeremy started building their audience right from the beginning.

The email and newsletter are the very first thing that Jeremy did and it's what I think every filmmaker should do when they initiate a project. You literally create a landing page. There are fantastic tools out there online that allow you to make a simple website. You just have your two sentence synopsis of what the project is and then join up to the main list and then you start growing from there.

One of the things that really helped the project along was some coverage by a couple of big websites. We're talking Huffington Post big!

There's a lot of things that helped us grow the main list from zero to about three thousand people when we launched. One of the big things that happened early on was Jeremy was testing the idea by making some short films and putting them up on Vimeo. One of those short films got picked up on Huffington Post. Jeremy wakes up and there were another three hundred people on the mailing list overnight.

But not all PR is created equal.

We did a big PR campaign. We were doing things like, Jeremy was doing TV appearances on Australian TV and when that went on air we were looking at our analytics on our website and it barely registered much of a bump. It's a very passive medium. When Yahoo Finance covered us and actually had a link at the end of their article to our website, it went ballistic and drove twenty thousand visitors to our site in just one day. That was really an interesting learning experience seeing how patchy PR can be. It's really hard to know, going into it, what's going to be better PR and what's worth and what's not worth it. I think you just got to go do as much as you can and then luck kind of takes over.

Working with bloggers was a core part of the Chris and Jeremy's strategy.

We really tried to make genuine friends with bloggers and other kinds of influential people in the tiny house world. There's probably half a dozen bloggers who between them had an audience of a hundred thousand or two hundred thousand people. So we just worked really hard to get them on board with our project and try and help them however we could with what they were doing and be part of that community. When the time came to launch we could actually call on them to do a blog article on us, cashing in that goodwill. I think that's the wonderful thing about the internet, there are real people on the other end and if you treat them with respect, if you actually make a genuine effort to create some event they would like and really reach out to them, then people can really engage with that.

It all takes time but if you do that whilst you're making the film and if you're authentic with what you're talking about it's great because it's something that Hollywood can't do. That's the one thing, the independent product that filmmakers have, is that we can actually be genuine and honest and we can just talk from our own voice and just use the internet as a way to get it out there.

Once they had some people on their mailing list what did the Small Is Beautiful team provide in terms of updates?

Video updates with Jeremy talking to camera about what his journey on making the film was as a first-time filmmaker. That was a story in itself of him struggling to get this film made and also using that list as a resource for help. Everything from finding places to stay and finding people to help.

Another unique aspect of the process for Chris and Jeremy was their media friendly cinema launch.

We built a pop-up cinema in a warehouse to launch the film and we ran our ticketing through Eventbrite and then we did a big public relations campaign to promote the event. We had, I think, about a thousand people in the first four days. We did a four-day launch. The great thing, when you run your own event like that, you get to have all the contact details of everyone who came because you can literally just download the contact list of everyone who came.

As well as gathering contact details, creating their own launch event meant that they had a media-ready story to tell.

We really worked to make the launch of the film an interesting story to do the media's job for them by giving them the story. We set up in a warehouse and we had a tiny house there for people to see. It was all very photogenic; we built a bar; we had DJs; we had food trucks. It was all really experiential. That was all designed to have a cool fun launch but also played the additional role of being very photogenic so the media could come down and do a story with all of this happening in the background.

The media doesn't just respond to a photogenic launch though, compelling and relevant subject matter also helps.

It comes back to that thing of thinking about a film that's actually going to really have a strong audience and people that are going to be interested in checking it out. In Australia and many parts of the world, we've got a massive housing affordability problem. The media has covered that to death and is desperately looking for a new angle on that story that's not going away. And so we come along and we got these really sexy photos of beautiful tiny houses and people talking about how this is a different way to live and to solve the housing affordability crisis. You've got to give the media value if you want to get value out of the media. Journalists don't get paid much and it's so hard to run a media company now so journalists are working hard and they don't have much time and if you can make their life easier for them by giving them a pre-made story it's a no brainer.

After the four night extravaganza, Jeremy and Chris took the movie on the road.

We commenced a one-month cinema tour through Tugg which is the Cinema on Demand platform. The great thing with Tugg is that you do it yourself and you get to keep all the data, you get to keep all the addresses. That was essential so that by the time we launched we had this critical mass of three thousand people as well as about fifteen hundred people on Facebook and other social media platforms. We just had this audience ready to launch the film to.

After the theatrical tour, it was time to launch online via Video on Demand.

Once it actually came time to put it up online, we were able to really go out with a big bang and start making money rather than just putting a message in a bottle on the internet which is a sea of messages in bottles. That's the big scary thing about putting stuff online, there's so much stuff out there. How do you make some noise?

And how did they make some noise?

41

Our whole strategy was about that one moment when we hit publish on the film. Everything needed to come together to drive as much traffic to that website as possible to get people to look. The people that had already seen the film in cinema, and on the cinema tour were essential because if they like the film they would talk about it with their friends. We could remind them to do that via asking them on email. That was a really big thing that drove more people to come see the film.

Where is Small Is Beautiful up to now?

The big thing that's happened in the last couple of months for the film was that we got a deal with Netflix. It went up on Netflix in Australia, America and Canada and Holland and the UK and New Zealand. I think it's going really well.

Read more about the strategy behind Small Is Beautiful on their wonderfully transparent article that lays out all the numbers for you to see for yourself. www.smallbeautifulmovie.com/blog/micro-budget-documentary-c

Watch the film on Netflix or via Video on Demand from www.smallbeautifulmovie.com

Belinda Mason

Chapter 6 Belinda Mason

I spoke to Belinda Mason about making the documentary Constance on the Edge. The first question I asked was, I get the impression that you had a relatively large team working with you for the documentary. How did you bring that team together?

It was actually a tiny core crew – just three of us for the shoot over a number of years. Producer, Marguerite Grey; Cameraperson/sound, Joanne Parker; and me. The majority of the time it was just Jo and me driving from Sydney to Wagga and filming for a few days. I think we did 12-15 trips to Wagga. The other key contributors to the documentary were Susan Danta, who came on before we started shooting so we could plan the style of the rotoscoped animation; Denise Haslem, our editor; and Antony Partos, composer.

The animated flashbacks are a striking feature of the film. What role did they play for you in telling the story?

Where no film footage existed to represent what Constance or Mary were speaking about we decided to use animation sequences to tell the story. This allowed us to weave the film with a rich seam of dreams and memories. Animation can evoke feelings and emotions that can't be spoken, allowing the audience to see beneath the surface.

The cinematography is beautifully constructed. The lighting, composition, movement – all work together to build compassion for Constance and her family. Were the subjects understanding of the requirements of a film shoot and the patience needed to build the right feel?

Constance was incredibly understanding and patient with us. We'd worked together before on a documentary called 'I'll Call Australia Home' so she was very comfortable in front of the camera. She'd had an experience in Kakuma Refugee Camp (in Kenya), where she spent 10 years---it was here she came to understand the power of film while volunteering as an interpreter for FilmAid.

FilmAid is an NGO that trucks in massive mobile screens to camps and screens a variety of films – anything from Charlie Chaplin to HIV-AIDS awareness films. Often they have audiences of over 10,000 people. Constance says, "when you're watching a film you forget that you haven't eaten for days".

I'm sure you had a lot of footage that ended up on the cutting room floor. How did you go about finding the story in all the footage you collected?

Like most observational documentaries we really 'wrote the script' in the editing room. Working with editor Denise Haslem, a master storyteller was a joy.

When you started filming Constance over ten years ago, did you have any idea where you were going with the story?

I directed Constance 10 years ago in 'I'll Call Australia Home' - a story about a refugee family arriving in Australia. It was a film full of hope. Then Constance contacted me a few years down the track and said things weren't working out for her in Australia. Seeing Constance at a point when she was in great emotional pain was shocking. She asked me to collaborate with her to share her experience of what it takes to belong in a new land far from home. What emerged as we filmed was that welcoming people from refugee backgrounds – even the smallest of gestures can make a difference - can promote or impede their ability to contribute successfully over the long term.

Did you get funding for post-production?

We were funded through Screen Australia and Screen NSW but the majority of our funding came through Good Pitch. Constance on the Edge was one of seven documentary films selected for the 2014 philanthropic Good Pitch2 Australia initiative. Good Pitch brings together filmmakers with foundations, not-for-profits, campaigners, philanthropists, policy makers, brands, educators, broadcasters and media to forge powerful alliances around documentary films that will have a significant impact in relation to issues of social importance.

At what stage did you develop a marketing strategy? Did that strategy pan out in the way you expected?

We developed an Impact Strategy in tandem with our distribution plan as we recognised that this was not a big cinema release film and we needed to find a successful model to market the film. We've been working with our partners in the refugee space to ensure a broad national audience sees the film. We sell screening licenses through our website and downloadable digital resources to ensure a brilliant screening. One or two people from the team often attend screenings and have a Q&A afterward. We've had over 100 community screenings around the country. Often organisations or individuals buy a screening license, hire a cinema and make it a big event – even a fundraiser. From feedback, we're finding it's starting conversations in country towns and helping to foster more welcoming communities for people from refugee backgrounds.

A documentary like this wears its heart on its sleeve and seeks to contribute positively to conversations about refugees in Australia. Do you build other resources into the distribution package to help facilitate that conversation?

Educational resources have been created for schools, and the team is working with police, torture and trauma services, local government and community services to build greater awareness amongst "first responders" – people who regularly interact with refugees and humanitarian entrants in their work, but do not necessarily understand refugee trauma and how it manifests.

You mentioned that you work alongside refugee partners and that community screenings are an important part of your distribution model, what does that look like on the ground?

The Refugee Council of Australia have chosen Constance on the Edge as the film to celebrate Refugee Week 2017 in June – this means we will have hundreds of screenings in libraries, councils, schools, community groups, and individuals.

After working with the footage for so long you must know it inside and out. Have you found that as audiences come to the story with fresh eyes they respond to things in the film that you didn't anticipate?

46

Many people have come up to us after the film, very emotional, and said something like, "that was my mother or father up there on the screen" - they explain that their parent was a Holocaust survivor; or a refugee from Vietnam; or a European migrant – and say, "but my father/mother was never able to talk about their experiences or feelings".
When we screen it to school kids – they adore Constance and start thumping their feet and cheering for her!

What are you working on now?

I'm in Israel now working on a film about the impact of trauma on societies.

To delve further into Constance on the Edge, hit the film website here...
www.constanceontheedge.com.

Ariana Bernstein

Chapter 7 Ariana Bernstein

Ariana is a filmmaker who works out of Brooklyn. In her own words, Ariana Bernstein is,

a screenwriter, a film producer, an executive producer, sometimes an actor when I really feel like it. I had two films that came out within two years of each other, Delusions of Guinevere as actor/co-screenwriter/co-producer and Fort Tilden which I executive produced.

And she is driven to produce films that aspire to,

make social change.

So does that mean she slogs it out in journalism or dominates the documentary film festival circuit?

Delusions of Guinevere and Fort Tilden both happen to be satires and dark comedies. I'm not exactly sure how it worked out that way but actually, dark comedies and satires seem like a really effective way of making social change. Not at the level that I anticipated but it's still at a really good level.

Which is why Ariana is working on a small screen comedy next.

I'm working on a series. We're not exactly sure where it's going to live. It's definitely going to be somewhere on the small screen either on the web or on the TV. It's called Peaked in High School. It's about three girlfriends from high school reuniting. They're in their thirties and they peaked in high school. Now they're trying to rebuild their lives from the shambles to see where they went wrong.

As well as following her passions into a project that she can't say too much about.

And then I'm working on something completely different which is a documentary. We are in development right now. We have some footage and we're going to be filming more this summer.

I can't say much about it at this point but I can say that it's about slavery and supply chains in all industries and it's very deep and heavy and sad. That's a very big catalyst for social change, which is something that I've always wanted to work on, something that could make a legislative difference.

So, into the marketing strategy. Ariana's first two films were both well received. One secured a theatrical release and the other is available on Video on Demand (VOD). So, has the marketing for these new projects started yet?

Not yet, we've been very focused on the scripts because we're trying to create masterfully, beautifully crafted scripts. I feel like we're behind on the social media front so I'm pushing to get that up and running. We have our names and we have everything parked for when we start but we need to start posting. I'm a firm believer in building your audience from the time you conceive a project however it's not always conducive to life or to how your work is unfolding. I feel like I need to focus so much on the script and the craft. It's hard to manage everything all at once.

Stop press! It seems that Ariana finds it as difficult as the rest of us to get all the ducks lined up for a creative social media marketing strategy. Is there also a fear that if you start building your audience when a project is still in development you are in danger of peaking too early?

I've had a few friends that have had films in early stages of development and they already have big Facebook fanbases and I always get updates if they're doing a Kickstarter or accepting donations. I get updates constantly like "thanks to… (and they tag somebody), for donating". That's great and that's a really important thing but it blocks up other people's news feeds so I think there's a fine line with how you facilitate updates. It's a good thing that you remind people that people are donating, that you're looking for money, that this project is still going but maybe do it in blocks. Like, "thanks to, (and then tag fifteen people who gave money)". I just think you have to be a little bit strategic about it so you don't piss people off. But you know what, you can always unfollow people or unlike the page. I don't think you'd lose too much of an audience. It's something to consider but I definitely think starting earlier, the earlier the better in most cases.

Although social media is all about the social, sometimes it can feel like work.

I'm actually having fun with Instagram. I always thought of social media as a chore, something I had to do, but Instagram is really fun for me. Yesterday, it was Dolly Parton's birthday and I posted a picture of her with pink and glitter and it made me so happy and I hope that it brings that joy to my followers. Actually, I despise that term, followers. I should call them my Instagram community because it does feel like a community, it's very interactive, you know. Followers just seem like, "I'm not Jesus, why are you following me"? It's kind of bizarre. I don't like that I'm a follower of someone, but it's just semantics. I do like community. I'll use that from now on.

We all have personal goals and rules for how we use social media, Ariana tries to,

post twice a day but then life happens and I don't, so I try and post at least once a day. I like to check out what my community is doing and interact with them a bit and post some stuff when I feel inspired. Some days I really try and push my work. I try not to be too pushy about it but definitely part of the purpose of having Instagram is building up a fan-base for my films. It's also about connection and reaching out and understanding. It's kind of cool to see how other people live. I like to post things that have some levity and sparkle and joy because I have a pretty cynical world view so I like to be reminded in pictures that the world can also be a beautiful place.

Skills are good. Everyone needs skills. Where did Ariana pick up her skills in marketing and promotions?

Delusions of Guinevere was with a boutique distribution company. We did most of the marketing. They taught us how to do it but we did it ourselves. Fort Tilden was different. When you're working with a bigger distributor they do it for you.
It was good to get both perspectives. I learned a lot about marketing. It was a crash course and it's good to be involved on the ground level and to be really interactive with your community.

Well, what did Ariana learn?

I didn't know anything about marketing. I learned about a/b, whatever it's called. a/b testing, that's like a basic, 101, everybody, even my dog knows what that is, but I didn't. Facebook is actually extremely useful. They've built this crazy technology, software/interface – I don't even know what to call it I just know how to do it. You can be so specific in who you target. You can say you want women in one zip code between 18 and 40 who have kids under 5; you can be that specific. That's a great way to target and not waste your money and not bother people who wouldn't ordinarily be interested in your film.

What is the aim of advertising on Facebook?

You're always trying to drive people from your Facebook page to your Instagram and your website and then sign up for your mailing list. That's how it is – the mailing list is still gold. And so all of this is meant to convert to email sign ups and then audience numbers. It's amazing for a filmmaker to have such a wide audience. It just makes it that much more complicated in terms of marketing. I wish I could tell you the surefire way of that's how you market to a broad audience but that's the difficulty too, I'm a filmmaker and I'm trying to understand this entire world that is foreign to me.

When it all gets too much, why don't you just pack it in, delete your Facebook account and start posting pictures of funny cats to Instagram?

I think what keeps me going day after day in the film industry is to create things that matter. That's always been my goal. I see what I've done so far and I'm proud of it and I see it also as a stepping-stone to get to where I want to be creatively. I have such a strong passion for telling stories about social change, about really important human stories that pull at your heartstrings and really make you change your perspective and your perception of the world.

Ariana can be found at www.buddhabellyprod.com

Vic Campbell

Chapter 8 Vic Campbell

Vic is a freelance writer and broadcaster based in Victoria, Australia. He produced the television documentary Forgiven People and is associate producer for the feature documentary Smithy. I asked him, where did you first get the idea for Smithy?

The Rev Dr. John 'Bullfrog' Smith has been called 'John Wesley on a motorbike' but Smithy, as he is affectionately known, is more than this. He has worn many hats – youth minister, evangelist, apostle, writer, theologian, teacher, media personality, social justice warrior, blues music lover, husband, father, grandfather... and biker.
Over two years in the making, 'SMITHY' is a feature length (130 mins) biographical film. It covers John's entire life from childhood to his recent battles with cancer but has a special focus on John's middle years from about the age of 20 to 40. This includes the seminal moment of his 'conversion' from conservative to radical and the period when he met his wife, Glena, had three children, founded God's Squad, became a media darling, established his ministry to schools and universities, and set up his radical church in the outer suburbs of Melbourne, Truth and Liberation Concern.

How did this project come about?

After working successfully with filmmaker Don Parham on a 30-minute doco for television, I suggested that "someone should tell John Smith's story before he dies".

Did you imagine a feature-length film right from the beginning and did you have an idea about how that could be funded?

Although most of Don Parham's previous docos for (the Australian media networks) the ABC and SBS were a 'television hour' in length, he definitely wanted the Smithy film to be 'feature length' from the outset. To maximize our creative freedom with the project we decided to crowd-fund and self-distribute the film. We thought that any broadcaster interest that might come down the track would pay for re-versioning the film for television.

Did you test the market before you began?

Not really. We knew that John had almost 5,000 'friends/followers' on Facebook and that he had a global profile that was especially strong in Australia, UK, and parts of Europe.

You ran two Pozible campaigns - one successful and one unsuccessful, can you tell us why you think there was a mixed response?

At one point, we considered going for broke with a $100,000 target in our first Pozible campaign but, because we were going to run an 'all or nothing' campaign, we decided it was safer to just aim for 'Stage 1' funding and set the target at half that amount. I think, in hindsight, this possibly created some confusion in our supporter group's eyes which contributed to the 2nd Pozible campaign failing.

How important was it for you to bring your crowdfunding audience along with you through production, post-production and finally into the release stage of the project?

Very important, as without our supporters the whole project would suffer. We attempted to keep donors informed through regular updates via Pozible and social media.

There are key communities that John has been involved with over the years; did you reach out to each of those communities individually?

Yes. Initially, we emailed our individual networks (i.e. personal contacts of the production team---there were 4 people on the team for the first stages of the project). Then we emailed church networks and 'arts' bodies such as the UK's Greenbelt Festival where John had had some involvement.

What techniques did you use to stay in touch with your audience? Did you maintain an email list? How often did you email your audience?

In the initial stages of seeking funds, we emailed our audience twice giving them an opportunity to support the project. We compiled an email list from our team member contacts and from John's own supporters (although this was a very small list).

Once the project was underway, we built a website dedicated to the film, created a Facebook page for 'SMITHY' the film and set up a blog to which we posted quotes from John's published books.

As you've moved closer to the launch date what have you done to make sure people know about Smithy?

Updated emails to donors via our Pozible site and daily posts (late in the day or early evening) on our Facebook page accompanied with a photo/still taken from the film. We also sent our personalized email Launch invitations to 'key people' from all our networks.

You've received some endorsements from celebrities like Bono and Tim Costello, how have you sourced those endorsements?

John knows Bono as a friend. We asked John to record a short video endorsement with Bono on a visit to Dublin. We emailed Tim Costello and others, sending them video links to view the whole film as well as a comprehensive Press Kit about the film.

How important was it to have John Smith endorse the film even in the development phase?

'SMITHY" is a biographical doco, very much built around a major interview Parham did with John by locking him up in a studio for two long days. The film couldn't have been made without John's co-operation and endorsement.

You've laid out your funding strategy very transparently in your Pozible campaigns. www.pozible.com/project/186155 It looks like you haven't found the support that you were seeking from film funding bodies. How have you made up the shortfall in funding and do you still hope to find a mainstream distributor for the film?

We're not looking for a mainstream distributor at this stage. It is very much a niche audience for this film and I'd say we know best how to reach it. The main consequence of the shortfall in funding was it forced us to reduce the scope of the project. Fortunately, we were still able to deliver a feature-length doco, as planned, but we couldn't cover John's whole life in depth. As it turned out, the Smith story has a very natural climax, and break point, at about age 40. Although the film does cover his whole life (Smith is now in his 70's), its main focus is on the first 40 years. Depending on how DVD sales go, we may look at doing a 'SMITHY 2' film.

Did you have a well-defined marketing strategy from the outset or has it evolved as you've moved from one stage of the project to another?

Our marketing strategy has evolved through different stages of the project. The positive reactions to our initial 'push' were very important in confirming to us that the project could proceed. The second campaign, although we didn't reach our target goal, encouraged us a little further. With the finished product, we will now explore other avenues of promotion.

Have you used social media at all? Do you feel that has been successful?

We have used Facebook extensively and we feel that this has certainly helped in creating an awareness of the crowdfunding efforts as well as keeping supporters and the public, in general, informed about the project's progress.

Have you used traditional PR methods and has that been successful?

Traditional PR methods such as sending out media releases to radio personnel and journalists have had some success resulting in phone interviews and printed newspaper and magazine articles prior to the film's release. The 23-second video from Bono resulted in a sizeable piece in Melbourne's Herald-Sun (about one-third of a page).

Have you set specific goals in terms of audience size or reach?

Not really. We attempted to reach as many of our own networks as possible combined with those people who were aware of John's activities.

SMITHY is available on DVD via www.parham-media.com

Claudia Pickering

Chapter 9 Claudia Pickering

Claudia is an Australian filmmaker who has done most of her work in the United States so far. For Claudia, one of the first audiences she considers is the actors.

Something that I did when I cast Frisky that I think was really crucial, I made sure I did the casting in a theatre. I knew how low budget the film was but I knew that I was going to actually finish the film. I've been on some decent budget films that people don't actually bother finishing. (You know who you are.) It breaks your heart to work on something for a year but then there's nothing to show for it. I know I'm going to pull through for these people. If I do a casting in my house they'll think it's this fly-by-night, crappy, little production that may not get made. I held it in a theatre, which was two hundred and fifty bucks or something to hold it there for the day. That was a chunk of my budget, but it was worth it because every single person there felt like they're part of something legit and we didn't have any flaking from the cast, which has gone on in the past. So that was money well spent.

Once the piece is made and you haven't had any cast pull out on you and the picture is finished, what do you do with it?

We did the San Francisco premiere in December. We're actually about to bring on board our marketing team (there's only one person on our marketing team!) to do our distributions that are due in the US in March or April and then in Australia. We already had a bit of an existing network because all of our cast and crew have got everyone in their networks. We reached out to a bunch of local publications and reporters and stuff in San Francisco because it is a really San Francisco-centric film. They all wrote articles about us. The press release that we did for it was in this very exciting language, without hyping it too much, "Shot in San Francisco and indie this and underground that". We tried to make a little spectacle of it. We also chose to screen it at a really independent film staple spot called the Roxie. The cinema itself was very helpful because they advertised for us to their existing network of people who give a damn about indie film.

The sheer energy that Claudia throws into all of her projects pays dividends on other projects! If you want somewhere to screen your film, why not start a film festival?

I run a little film festival out here in Sydney called FreshFlix. The reason we started it was so that my family and friends could see my (debut feature) film Frisky. It was a year after we'd made it and nobody had seen it. We have a mate who's got a house with a backyard that overlooks the ocean and then we just made a screen; we got the wood and got the fabric and stretched the screen. Then we made it into this whole event. We got a big red tablecloth and hand painted FreshFlix all over it. We gave it a name. Then I didn't want it to just be Frisky. I wanted to take the focus off it just a little bit. We put a thing on Film Freeway and invited people to submit their short films for free so that we could screen a handful before Frisky. We thought nobody will submit. This is a backyard Film Festival! In forty-eight hours we got five hundred submissions or something outrageous and we were going, "we've got to shut it down, shut it down". So we sat and watched a shit load of films.

That explains the inaugural FreshFlix but what's the excuse for the rest of them?

We had a whole bunch of mates and friends of friends that came as a result of that and people started talking about FreshFlix. So we did another one in a mate's warehouse in Redfern. He happens to have a big studio space because he's a photographer and his fiancé happened to have a Japanese food truck. So how convenient is that? We did that again and we started getting a name for ourselves and that has actually become a massive platform. Suddenly, you're creating this network of filmmakers and people who didn't know they give a shit about indie film but they do. They're like, "oh this is actually awesome". It's like going to a party and then you sit down and watch films and then you party again and it's great. For me, it's now become this huge platform. When I have work ready to go I have an enormous audience built in. I can say, "well, we're screening my film now" and everyone who already comes to our stuff says, "you guys always curate good films". That's a really, really awesome little bit of marketing.

I talk about social media a lot because I know that it can really help to get your work out to your audience. How does Claudia use the socials to boost her business?

I'm not very good at social media stuff. Jess and I who I do the FreshFlix stuff we're both like, "whoa OK, we'll do it, we'll try and post some stuff". I know a thing or two about blog posts and generating traffic and all that sort of thing. But nothing to me compares to actually building this community on the ground, which is really cool. I'm just all about actually making a real connection. There's nothing like having a bit of face-to-face time with people. The best thing to do is just be nice to people.

Let's hear a bit more about blog posts.

We're doing little things like we did a blog post about how to make a feature film for under five grand and we made an e-book about that. That way we're getting people's e-mail so that we can let them know when we've got shows that we want them to come to FreshFlix. We've got a really nice big email list now, which is great. It's all about the email list.

The final thing I talked about with Claudia was how important it is to have a great website.

It is a matter of just building up your stuff and having a bloody nice website. Every time I speak to different funding bodies and production companies they will be like, "you've got a really nice site. I saw your stuff and I really like your website; it's fun to look at".

These are the three things Claudia says are most important about a website.

Filmmaking is so subjective. You can't explain to someone how good you are or how worthy you are of their money. It's portfolio-based stuff. Don't just have a YouTube link. Make sure that you build a whole experience around what you are as a brand, as a filmmaker because that is so important.

Thing number one.

—

You need a really nice tight reel that doesn't necessarily conform. People are always saying the reel's got to be like this and this and this and it's got to show this and that. Before you go and look at what formats you think a reel should be, I say your work needs to look sweet. You have to be proud of every single thing that you put in there. You've got to decide what your brand is. The reel that you get when you hit my website is a comedy reel. It's a comedy filmmaking reel and people go, "oh man that's funny". You've got to say, "what is the thing that I want people to come away from that reel with? What will they like about my brand?" And make your reel around that. Don't pad it out with bullshit. If you're doing comedy make it about the funny moments and obviously make it look sleek and don't put something in that you don't like. If you're a director they care what kind of mood you're getting out of the whole thing. They want to come away with a feeling.

Thing number two

Money shots. People like really big imagery; it's just nice. Go to a gallery and tell me you're attracted to the tiny picture. You know you're not. You could literally blow up a picture of anything and sell it for a lot of money. People like big pictures. Film is a visual medium where you have to just suck people in with sexy visuals (I don't mean actual sexy unless that's your area). Suck 'em in with whatever is your vibe. Again, you do have to have a strong understanding of what your brand is. It's so important.

Thing number three

You need press. It doesn't even have to be press; it can be little things that other people have said. Using Donald Trump as the example you can say anything and if you've said it, it's kind of real. If you put things on your website that legitimise you people can't un legitimise you from that. Obviously, you've got to have a sneaky little bit of your resume and all of that, because people will want to see that but I don't think that should be front and center. So things like press, things like little quotes about you that people have said.

If you happen to have the odd famous person who may have said something about you, throw it on. I can't speak for anyone who is not doing comedy because that's what I do but I want to look like a serious filmmaker too, so people have said, "Great to work with", and, "hard worker", and, "great stuff". Then other people are like, "I roll with this chick because she's got balls". Why not throw them on because I do comedy I'm allowed to do stuff like that!

Take a look at everything Claudia is up to on her super on-message website with blown up images, quotes from real people, and a hot as reel. www.pickclaud.com

Dee McCullay

Chapter 10 Dee McCullay

Wildman Dee McCullay is a filmmaker, writer, and musician based in Canada. Hot off the back of his successful horror films, Border Patrol and Fallacious he has most recently...

been working on Scars: a paranormal dramatic horror short. It was originally a short story written by Dave Dubose, called Solution to Sadness, which I thought was great, and I knew there would be a film in it.

What is Scars about?

Scars is about a young girl named Faith Beckett. She is on her last legs and has done all she can to stay afloat. She has some mental health issues and has been hospitalized at times for cutting and trying to take her own life. The crescendo of her horrible life is, she goes home to find an eviction notice on her door. She doesn't realize it, but she has been followed by a guardian spirit for quite a while now, who has revealed herself, just in time to warn her that if she cuts again, it will be the last cut. Her life will be lost tonight should she go through with it. She is also confronted with a dark entity who opposes the first spirit and tries to convince her to go through with it.

That's an intense storyline. Is a shoot about such dark material difficult?

Problems surrounded the production as our actress playing the part of Faith Beckett had a minor accident on the way to pick up the other actors. By the time she made it over, the two decided to opt out of the film, as she was so late. The apartment was rented for the shoot and with all the preparations pre-made, we managed to find two other actors at, literally, the last minute. Then we lost our on location audio and had to leave everything to post-production ADR work.

Wow, that's not the material. That's just a succession of unfortunate events. Did everything go smoothly after that?

It was a very quick shoot from 8:30 pm to 12:30 am. I wasn't really sure what we had coming home from shooting that night. But after getting it to editing and starting to put things together, we had the beginnings of something great, something quite freaky and something intense.

Scars is Dee's third film in quick succession. How has he built up his business to this point?

I have worked on quite a few productions over the years. I created Thunderstryker Films in 2009, making free tourism videos to get my name out there and noticed, and it worked.

Tourism videos are quite different to Dee's other work. How did he transition into horror?

I went on to produce a show for local television called the Thunder Bay Paranormal Society, consisting of 3 episodes. From there I took the paranormal into a new realm in my own show made for television called Dark History, investigating paranormal locations with orbit and tragic histories using Spirit Radio Communication (my own branding), Electronic Voice Phenomenon, and video.

And did that open up other opportunities?

Dark History took me into the states to work with Chelsea Damali of A&E Bio Channel's Haunted Encounters Face to Face. From there, I came back to Canada to continue on making Dark History episodes. The show was not picked up by executives but is available on YouTube. From there I decided to write some screenplays, Fallacious was produced in April 2016 and released October 10, 2016. Andy Van Scoyoc's, Border Patrol was shot over one month and released November 24, 2016. Both films received a lot of praise and acclaim. Scars was released December 27, 2016, and has been nominated for the iHorror Awards 2017, and is an official selection of the Stormy Weather Horror Fest.

How does Dee build his audience?

I promote my work on Twitter and Facebook, where most of my

work gets shared by fans and friends who continue to support me. My Twitter audience has grown from 1,200 to 7,700 since October because of the horror shorts I have made and continues to grow with the release and success of these short films. I only use Facebook and Twitter to promo all my work and so it all depends on followers and friends to help by sharing. It's hard to get someone to click but things are getting better with being seen and heard. For a while, I felt like there was no one out there watching or listening. But today I am getting seen and heard.

Dee has seen much success with his films but there isn't much money in shorts. How does he sustain himself and his creativity?

Most of my work has not made any profit but I have had paid gigs in the past where I have produced work for tourism and municipalities. Currently, I have been requested for audio work for a museum. I love history. Aside from that, I have just monetized my YouTube platform, but I don't expect much income from it yet.

What's the idea behind monetizing YouTube?

I started my YouTube channel in early 2010. Back then I just wanted to be seen. These days, I definitely need the money to keep producing my films as it all comes out of my own pocket (I have not gone onto crowdfunding… yet), and funding from views would be a good way.

Does Dee have a brand or a way of positioning himself online?

I present myself as a weirdo, the guy you think is hilarious and weird, whom you can't take your eyes off as you don't know what he will do next. My tweets are both horror and hilarious. I like to keep people entertained as a horror head. Followers learn quickly that I like to be a weird person, and my films are on a level of genius. I thank all my supporters and make newcomers feel welcome.

What about business goals or life goals? Does Dee set targets and track how he is tracking towards those targets?

I believe my true mission is to become famous. The key to fame is don't stop, just keep waking and doing what you love, and become the best you can be and one-day people will take notice of your talents. Don't give up. I am very positive, even though I write some terribly evil, outlandish screenplays. If being weird leads me into some actual money so be it, as I work hard daily to become famous.

Does Dee have any final words for up and coming filmmakers?

I would say if you are getting into film the way I did, bypass school and just go for it... it's a tough life. There is no guild. It's sheer will and determination. It's getting up in the morning and being a do-er. It's looking at your work and criticizing it to death and continually striving to make it better or top it. Never give up on the dream. Just don't stop.

Chase down Dee on Twitter and Facebook.
www.twitter.com/dee_mccullay
www.facebook.com/DeeMcCullay/

About the author and editor

Nathan March publishes magazines, books, blog articles, tweets, and videos in the service of creative people everywhere. He works from a shared creative studio in the leafy city of Adelaide, Australia, and has an extensive background in filmmaking and theatre. To find more resources to help you build a sustainable creative practice, visit www.followmagazine.online

www.ingramcontent.com/pod-product-compliance
Lightning Source LLC
Chambersburg PA
CBHW021018180526
45163CB00005B/2006